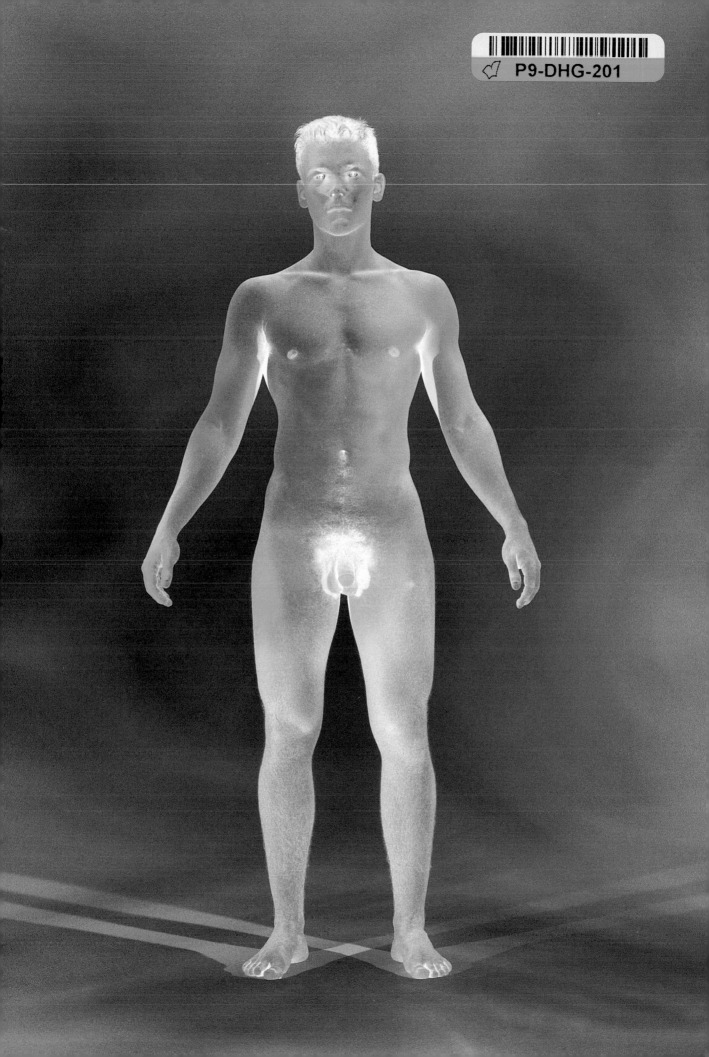

LYLE ASHTON HARRIS, ECSTACY #2, 1987—89 (NOT IN EXHIBITION)

ROBERT FLACK/LYLE ASHTON HARRIS/DENIS LESSARD

IN THIS WORLD

Curator
Keith Wallace

CONTEMPORARY
ART GALLERY

Vancouver Canada

In the Western world there are various systems at work that determine the norms for sexual identity. These systems conform to church/state ethics, to medical science and, not surprisingly, to the mass media. The first provides the moral/legal parameters, the middle a biological or pathological subtext, and the last, models that exemplify the representative male and female. Both gay men and lesbians have been and still are clearly out-of-sync with the societal expectations implicit within these systems. And though there are many shared concerns regarding homosexuals, there are also inherent differences surrounding male and female sexuality. This exhibition focuses on issues being explored by gay men; indeed, any examination of male sexuality has been notably absent except within the gay male realm. Through the language of photographic images, Robert Flack, Lyle Ashton Harris and Denis Lessard have cleared a space for the expression of gay male sexual identity within the North American cultural construct.

Before considering how these three artists tackle sexual identity, I want to look at some of the conditions that govern images pertaining to gay men. Before the latter part of the 1960s, overt representation of homosexuality in any form was rare; throughout the 1970s, it was openly discussed and considerably more visible, primarily in literature and film. But, by the late 1980s, art exhibitions showing the gay male body—*Robert Mapplethorpe: The Perfect Moment* in the U.S.A., *Evergon 1971–1987* in Canada and *Ecstatic Antibodies* in Britain—set off alarm bells in the minds of those who are opposed to homosexuality and its validation in mainstream society.[1]

In these exhibitions, photographs of the male body illustrated an avowal of desire between men that did not sit comfortably with the prevalent heterosexual code of ethics. Fear was aroused and questions ensued as to whether these works constituted art or pornography.[2] That many of these photographs depicted homosexuality's more forbidding aspects—from sadomasochism to AIDS, neither of which, incidentally, are limited to sexual relations between men—further angered the forces of intolerance. To some detractors, this artwork catered to special interest groups; to others, such images were capable of poisoning public standards of decency. The integrity, ethics and artistic responsibility of the hosting institutions were also questioned, demonstrating that even those providing a forum for the examination of homosexual images could also be implicated in anti-gay campaigns. That *Ecstatic Antibodies,* after its initial showing, was deemed an undesirable risk by other exhibition venues led to a premature termination of its touring schedule.[3] Moreover, that both

1 The Corcoran Gallery in Washington, D.C. cancelled the Mapplethorpe exhibition in 1989; the Mendel Art Gallery in Saskatoon was challenged by City Hall, one of its main funding sources, in 1990 for showing Evergon; the municipal art gallery in Salford banned *Ecstatic Antibodies* in 1989.

2 A similar incident occurred in Vancouver in 1984 with Paul Wong's video installation *Confused: Sexual Views,* a work which showed interviews with couples of all sexual persuasions. Upon seeing the videos just days before the opening, the then director of the Vancouver Art Gallery deemed the work "not art".

3 The exhibition evolved into the book, *Ecstatic Antibodies; Resisting the AIDS Mythology,* edited by Tessa Boffin and Sunil Gupta, (London: Rivers Oram Press, 1990).

4 An exception would be the many Gay Pride Day celebrations that occur across North America where safety in numbers allows such acts.

5 In 1974 the American Psychiatric Association finally removed homosexuality from its diagnostic manual of sicknesses.

the director of the Contemporary Arts Center in Cincinnati and the institution itself were charged with two obscenity counts for exhibiting *The Perfect Moment* (they fought them and won) demonstrates just what volatile territory we are addressing.

The protests these exhibitions incited is symptomatic of an attitude that wishes to deny homosexuality a public presence. Although homosexuals experience more 'freedom' today than at any time during the past century, integration into the mechanics of society is far from complete. In 1969, the Canadian government passed Bill C-150 which removed consensual sex between same-sex partners from the Criminal Code. The anticipation of legalized homosexuality was exhilarating for many gay men and lesbians who had previously lived illegal lives, and the early 1970s marked the beginning of a vocal era of 'gay liberation' and an openness towards all forms of sexuality. Why is it, then, that twenty years later, two men simply holding hands or kissing each other in public remains a taboo, an act of defiance?[4] Furthermore, why is a long-standing relationship between two men or two women not recognized legally as are those of heterosexual common-law couples? Liberal sentiments do not necessarily achieve social change. ● Attitudes hostile to homosexuality persist for many reasons, yet two seem to predominate. One stems from a chronic perceptual hangover that the homosexual is deviant and degenerate; a legacy inherited from pseudoscientific studies during the last century that linked homosexuality to insanity. Until quite recently, homosexuality was considered a sickness in need of a cure: it did not fit in with the gender designations that comprise 'normal' sexual and social behaviour so it was assumed that something had gone awry.[5] The word *homosexual* was not even in usage until the late 19th century. ● Another reason is expressed by religious fundamentalists who consider the homosexual a messenger of moral decay and a contributor to the breakdown of the family unit. Hard economic times or social disarray often generate a rise in fundamentalist movements whose influence cannot be dismissed. Most fundamentalist ideologies, and there are many around the world, see society as a totalized entity in which behavioural differences function as a threat to regulatory ideological agendas. In addition, fundamentalist groups are generally well versed in the power of the image, as exemplified by the popularity of televangelism. Perhaps this is why images of the gay male stimulate fear in the fundamentalist order; they recognize that photographs can tell conflicting truths.

In the past decade, a questioning of the photograph as a factual document has been the subject of debate in the visual arts. Objectivity and truth in the photograph have come under fire. The photographer chooses the image, the cropping and the caption, thereby manipulating a reading. Although the images in the Mapplethorpe and Evergon exhibitions were clearly staged, they nevertheless illustrated the power of the photograph to portray gripping illusions of the real, illusions capable of provoking strong homophobic reactions. Both artists relied heavily on the conventions of fine art photography and painting, and the content was, and is, considered by many to be more aesthetic than political. But, because of the censorship debates, it has turned out that any image which even suggests the gay male body has become a political image.

So it comes as no surprise that within the contradiction of having been granted legal status yet simultaneously encountering barriers to fully realize this status, the gay male intellectual/artist has taken on the challenge of finding ways to explore male sexuality. With the continued suppression of our visibility as positive contributors to society, gay men are reflecting upon who we are and where we are positioned in society.[6] For some twenty-five years women have been actively examining how they are represented in the mass media and how their bodies are subjected to the systems of patriarchy. This has partially been necessitated by a surfeit of images of women made by men. Yet, ironically, men's bodies have been virtually invisible except within a gay subculture. With little sign of inclusion in the mass of visual information that greets us daily, the gay male can only imagine his place within this heterosexually dominant world.

[6] This suppression has been exacerbated by mass media stories that emphasize gay life as one of child abuse and AIDS.

The vehicles of literature, film and, more recently, video, have been at the forefront of affirming the presence of homosexuality. As recently as thirty years ago, homosexual novels carried narratives with subtle underlying subtexts to be decoded by those "in the know". Now there are bookstores devoted to gay literature (and in some cities being fire-bombed for being so) and veiled narratives are a thing of the past. So far as censors are concerned, the written word is safe territory—readers can choose whether or not to visualize the often steamy descriptions within the privacy of their own minds. Censorship of books such as William Burrough's *Naked Lunch* or Hubert Selby Jr.'s *Last Exit to Brooklyn* now seem incredulous propositions. Such battles have been handed over to the visual image.

Since the advent of photography as the most efficient means of disseminating information, film has proven to be the most effective way of ushering the homosexual into visibility. Prior to the late 1960s, the homosexual in film was alluded to in a way that, like the early novels, was never explicit. In 1961, the Motion Picture Association of America fought to have the word *homosexual* cut from the British film *The Victim*. But that same year, the Motion Picture Production Code was liberalized to allow homosexual material on the screen and, by 1968, the homosexual increasingly became the main subject of films such as *The Sergeant, The Boys in the Band* and *Fortune and Men's Eyes.* I clearly remember the rising tension in the theatre when Rod Steiger grabbed John Philip Law and kissed him smack dab on the mouth in *The Sergeant.* The fact that it was Rod Steiger, who so often played tough guys, was all the more shocking. However, even though Steiger played the sergeant, a man in a position of power, he was also considered a victim unable to cope with his "strangeness" and committed suicide, a common fate for homosexuals in films.[7] This was one way of including homosexual subject matter without condoning it. Rarely did film empower the homosexual. The homosexual as victim, especially now that we are identified with AIDS, has remained the prevailing role. Generally, it has been gay filmmakers such as Stephen Frears (*My Beautiful Laundrette*) and Isaac Julien (*Young Soul Rebels*) who have brought forth images that both empower and acknowledge the complexities of the gay male. This move has also been reflected in video by artists like John Greyson, Richard Fung and Marlon Riggs. Even though video most often caters to specialized audiences, thereby allowing for more subjective and experimental approaches to gay content, some of this work has been receiving airtime on the Public Broadcasting System in the United States.

In recent years, the visual arts have become a potent arena in which to confront the negativity and invisibility of the gay male in society. Yet visual representation of the male body remains a troublesome issue as exemplified by Mapplethorpe *et al.* Efforts have been made to curtail homosexual imagery. In Britain, the passing into law of Clause 28 in 1988 prohibited any institution from promoting what might be deemed homosexuality. In the United States, an amendment was introduced to the National Endowment for the Arts bill in 1989 that restricted funding for the exhibition of any homoerotic material that the NEA might consider obscene or without artistic merit.[8] This amendment was largely provoked by photographic images of the gay male body and provided an efficient means of censorship. While such images have found acceptability in the pedestrian arena of the movie theatre, their presence in museums and galleries, where society's highest cultural values are legitimated and displayed, is evidently considered more problematic by those in power. Moreover, the images in film and video are ephemeral whereas those in photographs are open to prolonged visual examination.

It is within this context of the power of the image, of the perception of the gay male body as threatening, and of homosexual invisibility that I would like to consider the work of the artists in this exhibition. Their work is not "gay" art. Rather, Denis Lessard, Lyle Ashton Harris and Robert Flack examine masculinity from a gay male perspective within an often hostile world. Each offers different, and personal, investigations into what constitutes identity, implying that even though there is a collective sense of injustice, there is not necessarily any consensus as to what homosexual desire or identity actually is.[9] The singular, stereotypical idea of a homosexual is a fiction; there are class, racial and cultural distinctions as well as sexual complexities that include bisexuality and transsexuality.

7 Vito Russo, *The Celluloid Closet: Homosexuality in the Movies,* (New York: Harper & Row, 1985), pp.167–170.

8 In this amendment, homoerotic was tossed in the same camp as sadomasochism and sexual exploitation of children.

9 Simon Watney, *Policing Desire: Pornography, AIDS and the Media,* (Minneapolis: University of Minnesota Press, 1987), p.25.

Celuy qui se plaint de nature, dequoy elle a laissé l'homme
sans instrument à porter les senteurs au nez, a tort; car elles
se portent elles mesmes. Mais à moy particulierement, les
moustaches, que j'ay pleines, m'en servent. Si j'en approche
mes gans ou mon mouchoir, l'odeur y tiendra tout un jour.
Elles accusent le lieu d'où je viens. Les estroits baisers de
la jeunesse, savoureux, gloutons et gluans, s'y colloyent
autresfois, et s'y tenoient plusieurs heures après.

Montaigne

Le parfum de l'homme nouveau qui ose,
créé pour l'homme sophistiqué d'aujourd'hui:
confiant, dynamique, en constante recherche
de nouvelles frontières à conquérir.

Nor is homosexuality the only aspect of identity that interests these artists. Instead, it is one issue, albeit a major one, that they must grapple with while developing an understanding of their larger relational identity within society. Because homosexuals have been forced to develop their identity within a subculture, it is through a mirroring against the dominant culture that this identity takes form. The codes of masculinity are all around us, but they don't necessarily represent *us*.

Denis Lessard examines the position of being gay in relation to the various incarnations of men—and in turn masculinity—that circulate within the mass media. He has gradually assembled an archive of images that span a variety of genres and eras: from ad icons such as the Marlboro man, to postcards of men depicted in historical painting and sculpture, to entertainment personalities such as Tom Selleck and Jack Nicholson. What is interesting about Lessard's work is the absence of overtly gay references in the images he collects. Rather, he extracts through his presentation an underlying reading of how a gay man might perceive particular pictures of men differently from a "straight" man. As the representation of gay men is a rare occurrence in the mass media, such images are then susceptible to an interpretive reconstruction by the homosexual gaze.

Lessard's large wall arrangement of found images and texts, *Un mur d'hommes*, is a notice-board of various signs of masculinity. The nine framed texts—with quotations by Walt Whitman, Gabrielle Roy, Mu-mon and Montaigne among others—comment on some aspect of masculinity, from the pointed question "What is a man anyhow?" to a brief treatise on the moustache. Positioned to form an arched gate or opening, these framed texts have altarlike clusters of images placed around them. As such, the meaning of one image ricochets off the others. For example, the magazine advertisement showing two men facing each other in their Schiesser underwear presents a scenario which might carry imagined erotic meanings for the gay male whereas, for the heterosexual male, the ad might merely function as a showcase for underclothing. This gets complicated by photographs and reproductions of historical paintings and drawings placed in close proximity that depict various male couplings whose gaze is equally ambiguous. Other clusterings, such as the four portraits of men on record covers, some of whom softly look out at the viewer, seem empathic to the gaze returned by the homosexual. Still other, roughly thematic, clusterings focus on images of artists, of warriors, of Canada. In the centre of this whole construction, placed like a keystone, is a photograph of a male and female couple from a non-Western culture. They act as a counterpoint to remind us that other worlds exist outside the one Lessard has offered in this piece.

In *Série Marlboro*, Lessard has focussed on the depiction of the Marlboro man as a ubiquitous and subliminal personification of masculinity. Unlike Richard Prince's appropriated photographs of this legendary icon, which are rephotographed, cropped and enlarged to focus on the micro-gestures of the solitary man in a mythic past, Lessard uses actual magazines and finds irony in the placement of this 'lonesome cowboy' relative to other images within a single edition. When displayed open, a 1989 *Newsweek* magazine features on its front cover the headline "Gay America" and shows two men affectionately arm in arm; the back cover finds a tough Marlboro man who looks the other way. Lessard has taken other magazines and opened them to combine Marlboro man ads with covers such as one found in an issue of *Gentleman's Quarterly* touting Sean Connery as "The Last Real Man in America". Encased in plexiglass shaped to the form of the open magazine, these pages are presented like cultural artifacts. The objectifying of images in *Un mur d'hommes* and *Série Marlboro* is a positioning of the gay male within an arena where we are, for the most part, excluded. Although some of the images and texts seem cryptic, and indeed they are personal to the artist, Denis Lessard has created a visual and textual network that provides a space for both the artist and the viewer to investigate the floating nature of identity.

While Lessard situates himself relative to ready-made images that circulate in the dominant culture, Lyle Ashton Harris turns to himself, his family and his friends for subject matter with which to interrogate that culture. For Harris, "the autobiographical is a means of self-empowerment."[10] Thus he is invested with authority over self-representation, and through this, over the exploration of identity. This authority is necessary in order for gay men—and, in Harris' case, Black gay men—to assume a voice within society. However, Harris also speaks of the ambivalence that is inherently a part of this process: of engendering an interrogation which can be both liberating and painful, revealing his strengths and his vulnerabilities. His is an exploration into contradictory and often unexplainable aspects of the self, with the photograph becoming the stage for enacting this exploration.

The construction of gender and racial roles is the subject of a series of photographs in which Harris plays with the ideas of masquerade. In the triptych, *Americas,* Harris has positioned himself within a multiplicity of sexual/racial codes. Homosexuals have no paradigmatic codes for sexual identity; rather, we are free to negotiate our sexuality around the dualism of male and female. Adorning his nude male body with a blonde 'Marilyn' wig, beauty mark, and white face (the reversal of 'black face' comedians), Harris projects an image of male, female, black, white, stud and queen. In the left panel, "Miss Girl", he wears a stern, pouting expression that seems to ask the viewer, "Do you have a problem with this?" Pairing himself with a Black woman in the middle panel, "Kim, Lyle and Crinoline", Harris emphasizes the fluid gender space that he is inhabiting in these images and the constructed codes that determine feminine and masculine. In solidarity, both gaze back at the viewer who has entered their shared space. In the right panel, "Miss America", a Black woman draped in the American flag confronts 'the American dream', the idea of a nation or society that ideologically assumes itself a cohesive entity. Placing Black subjects at the centre of popular culture in order to change the dominant meanings is a strategy used by a number of Black photographers.[11]

10 Lyle Ashton Harris, "Revenge of a Snow Queen," *Out/Look,* (San Francisco, California), Spring 1991, p.9.

11 David A. Bailey, "Photographic Animateur, The Photographs of Rotimi Fani-Kayode in Relation to Black Photographic Practices", *Third Text,* No.13, (Winter 1990/1991), p.60.

DENIS LESSARD, <u>SÉRIE MARLBORO</u>, 1990—92

However, Harris' critique is not dismissive. Rather, he advocates social change by opening up a space for a multiplicity of selves that allows for greater manoeuverability within the ideological systems that are in place.

This multiplicity and ambivalence is further explored in a more recent work, *As he threw his golden hair over his broad brown shoulders. . . .* A large grid consisting of Polaroid portraits of himself, family and friends is interspersed with other Polaroids of still lifes and gay pornography. Here Harris employs a form of realism that is suggested by the candid moments characteristic of Polaroid photographs. The small scale of the Polaroids draw the viewer in to closely inspect the content. Personal notations identifying names and dates are written on some of the Polaroids and many of those photographed return the gaze of the viewer, who is then challenged to acknowledge that such worlds can and do coexist. The accompanying interweaving texts, one by Stuart Hall and the other by Harris, question the myth of 'inner wholeness', a wholeness that denies the many selves that comprise the self that each of us thinks we are.

Robert Flack considers the gay male body in a more metaphysical way. He pictures the body as a vessel containing energy centres that empower the body and mind in quite a different way than the North American male in an empowered state is often depicted. Power for Flack does not suggest the aggressive, often violent, 'protector' of established systems so prevalent in action films but, instead, is an ethos directed towards visualization of an exalted physical state.

His full-figured photographs, for example, present the male body as unabashedly beautiful and counteract the common idea of the homosexual body as helplessly diseased. In *The Light That Is A River Flowing,* Flack has superimposed an outline of the caduceus, a winged staff with intertwining serpents, whose symbolic roots lie in India, Egypt, Phoenicia and Ancient Greece, that today signifies the medical profession. The serpents are represented by bursts of light that coil across the body and symbolically promote the harmonious and healing union of opposites. The coils meet at vertical points along the body which have been activated into flames that, like the staff of the caduceus,

Last night I had a dream
"The search for the object of desire
that I was being fucked by this beautiful big Black man.
is not governed, therefore, by physiological needs,
He was tall, dark and rough.
but by the relationship to sign or representation.
He tried to enter my ass several times
It is the organization of these representations
but my hole was too tight.
that constitutes fantasy.
Finally, after several unsuccessful positions,
Desire is
he ordered me to stand up and assume doggy position.
a relationship
He thrust his dick into me
to fantasy."
and rode my tight mancunt.

LYLE ASHTON HARRIS, THE SECRET LIFE OF A SNOW QUEEN: THE VITRINE, 1990 (NOT IN EXHIBITION)

"The struggle to live within multiple locations and
As he threw his golden hair
to sustain multiple strategies of resistance
over his broad, brown shoulders
are allowed to invade
Miss Girl wondered
the mythical 'inner wholeness' of the self-image."
where this road would lead.

LYLE ASHTON HARRIS, <u>AS HE THREW HIS GOLDEN HAIR OVER HIS BROAD BROWN SHOULDERS...</u>, 1990

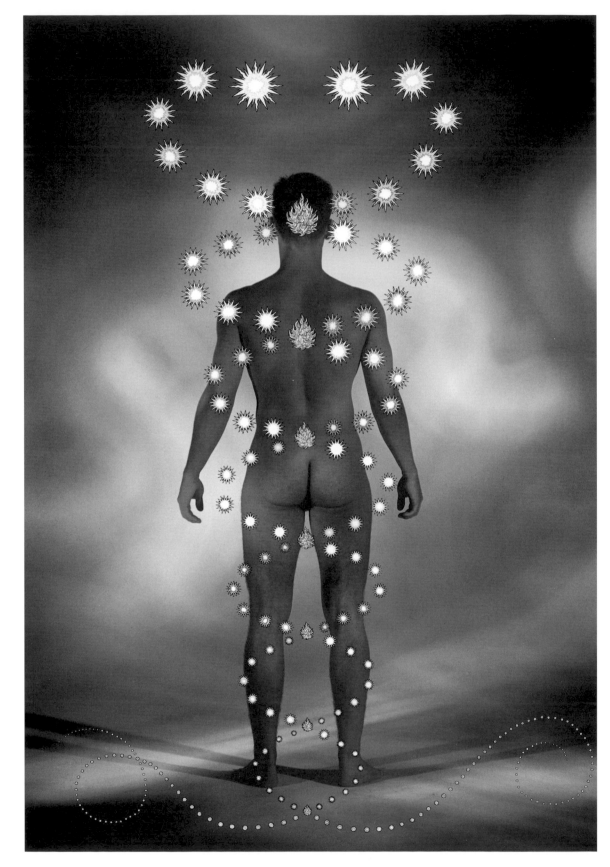

ROBERT FLACK, <u>THE LIGHT THAT IS A RIVER FLOWING</u>, 1990—91

represent power. Another image, *Anatomical Garden,* pictures the body as a network of roots mapping out the nervous system and emerging from the top of the head as a bouquet of flowers.

Love Mind pairs auroral abstract patterns with sections of the male body that correspond to each of the seven chakras—the perineum, the genitals, the navel, the heart, the throat, the forehead and the crown of the head. The chakras are energy centres in the body that, when activated by Tantric meditation, promote unity of body and mind. The abstract portions have hand-painted overlays of vortices, spoked wheels and circles that respond to *spiralling, rotating* and *radiating,* words used to describe the chakras when activated. The fragments of body are bathed in radiating colour projections mimicking a state of ecstatic visualization. Sexuality in this work is also correlated with the energy centres. The erect penis is, like the heart and the forehead, one of the main chakras in the male body. In Flack's images the body is seen as an organism reaching for the metaphysical, an organism that represents zones of empowerment rather than zones of impropriety.

In many respects the examination of same sex issues has arisen from a feminist paradigm of critiques discussing sexual difference and woman as "other" within a patriarchal society. Women's insistence upon respect and a position of empowerment has ruptured, but not yet overcome, the ingrained patriarchal consciousness that has placed all other 'sexualities' as submissive to heterosexual male prerogatives. This rupture has also made space for gay men and lesbians to assert their own voices, calling for a visible place in this world. Robert Flack, Lyle Ashton Harris and Denis Lessard do this by mobilizing the power of photographic images to enable a negotiation for more embracing and generous attitudes towards all sexual identities.

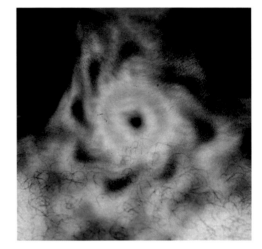

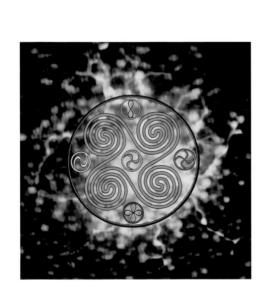

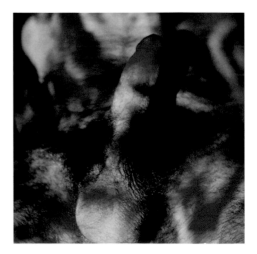

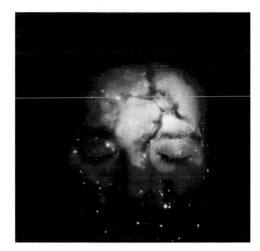

LIST OF WORKS IN EXHIBITION

ROBERT FLACK

Etheric Double, 1990–91
c-print
101.6 cm x 76.2 cm
courtesy Garnet Press Gallery, Toronto

The Light That Is A River Flowing, 1990–91
c-print
101.6 cm x 76.2 cm
courtesy Garnet Press Gallery, Toronto

Anatomical Garden, 1990–91
c-print
101.6 cm x 76.2 cm
courtesy Garnet Press Gallery, Toronto

Love Mind, 1992
10 c-prints
26.7 cm x 27.9 cm each
courtesy Garnet Press Gallery, Toronto

LYLE ASHTON HARRIS

Americas, 1988–89
three silver mural prints
152.4 cm x 101.6 cm each
courtesy the artist

*As he threw his golden hair over his
broad brown shoulders . . . ,* 1990
sx-70 polaroids, texts by Stuart Hall and
Lyle Ashton Harris
approximate dimensions 149.4 cm x 151.1 cm
courtesy the artist

Last night I had a Dream . . . , 1990
mirrored plexiglass with black silkscreen
text by Jeffrey Weeks and
Lyle Ashton Harris
24.7 cm x 24.7 cm
courtesy the artist

DENIS LESSARD

Un mur d'hommes, 1990–92
photograph, collected images, framed texts,
objects, pine and plywood, lettering
approximate dimensions 305 cm x 365 cm
courtesy the artist

Série Marlboro, 1990–92
magazines, cigarette package, plexiglass cases
approximate dimensions 39 cm x 142 cm
courtesy the artist

ROBERT FLACK

The evolution of this artwork is concerned with the sensory flow of the self and its inner sources of energy, to sexualize and spiritualize the body and the mind and use their regenerative powers towards healing both physically and psychically.

ROBERT FLACK
Born in 1957
Lives and works in Toronto

EDUCATION

1984 Computer Graphics Diploma, Sheridan College, Oakville, Ontario.

1980 BFA, Honours, York University, Toronto, Ontario.

SOLO EXHIBITIONS

1992 Galerie Rizzo, Paris, France.
Love Mind, Feature, New York, New York.
Love Mind, Garnet Press Gallery, Toronto, Ontario.

1991 *Empowerment,* Garnet Press Gallery, Toronto, Ontario.

1990 *Empowerment,* Feature, New York, New York.

1988 Plug-In Gallery, Winnipeg, Manitoba.

1987 *Love Magic Radiates,* Cold City Gallery, Toronto, Ontario.

1986 *Rob Sends His Love Magic To You!,* Niagara Artist's Centre, St. Catherines, Ontario.

1985 *Robert Flack's Heavy Vibes,* YYZ, Toronto, Ontario.

GROUP EXHIBITIONS

1992 *Tattoo Collection,* Air de Paris, Nice, France.

1991 *Union Language,* Mercer Union, Toronto, Ontario.
Light Sensitive, Academie en Rose, Garnet Press Gallery, Toronto, Ontario.
Parts: Robert Flack, Dyan Marie, Brian Scott, Galeria Carles Poy, Barcelona, Spain (catalogue). Toured to Centre Culturel Canadien, Paris, France.
Outrageous Desire, Rutgers University, New Brunswick, New Jersey.

1990 *AIDS Timeline,* Wadsworth Atheneum, Hartford, Connecticut.
Godhead, Feature, New York, New York.

1989 *Cold City/Vancouver Exchange,* Or Gallery and Contemporary Art Gallery, Vancouver, British Columbia.
Homogenius, Mercer Union, Toronto, Ontario (catalogue).
Cold City Artists, Cold City Gallery, Toronto, Ontario.
Robert Flack/David Rasmus, Cold City Gallery, Toronto, Ontario.

1988 *Walls on Fire,* YYZ, Toronto, Ontario.
Cold City Artists, Cold City Gallery, Toronto, Ontario.

1987 *At The Threshold: Representation and Identity,* S. L. Simpson Gallery, Toronto, Ontario (catalogue).
Split Surface: Robert Flack, David Horsley, Carolyn White, S. L. Simpson Gallery, Toronto, Ontario.
Hallwalls/YYZ Exchange, Hallwalls, Buffalo, New York.
Medium Photocopy, Saidye Bronfman Centre, Montreal, Quebec (catalogue).

1986 *Quick Draw,* Gallery 76, Toronto, Ontario.
Inaugural Exhibition, Cold City Gallery, Toronto, Ontario.
The State of Being, Canada Pavillion, Expo 86, Vancouver, British Columbia.
People, Places and Things, YYZ, Toronto, Ontario.
Medium Photo Copy, Rols Glasmeier Studio, Stuttgart, West Germany.

1985 *Doppelganger/Cover,* Aorta, Amsterdam, Netherlands.
Project Colourxerox, Visual Arts Ontario, Toronto, Ontario.
Videotex Retrospective, A Space, Toronto, Ontario.

1984 *Canadian Artists & Telidon,* Video Culture '84, Toronto, Ontario.
Toronto Drawing, Wynick/Tuck Gallery, Toronto, Ontario.
Desire, Gallery 101, Ottawa, Ontario (catalogue).

1983 *Flack/Stathacos,* Kingston Artists' Association Inc., Kingston, Ontario.
Unaffiliated Artists Show, S. L. Simpson Gallery, Toronto, Ontario.
Artists Books, Lunami Gallery, Tokyo, Japan.
Artists Books, Artist Space, Sydney, Australia.
Chromaliving, ChromaZone, Toronto, Ontario.

1982 *Celebration: Artists Doing It Downtown,* A.R.C., Toronto, Ontario.
Flack/Stathacos, ChromaZone, Toronto, Ontario.
YYZ Monumenta, Gallery 76, Toronto, Ontario.
O KromaZone: Die Anderen Von Kanada, Das Institut Unzeit, West Berlin (catalogue).

1981 *ChromaZone Chromatique,* ChromaZone, Toronto, Ontario.

SELECTED BIBLIOGRAPHY

Aletti, Vince. "Choices." *The Village Voice,* July 3, 1990, p.100.

Buchanan, Hamish. "Robert Flack, Empowerment." *Views,* Vol.8, No.2, (May 1991).

Crowston, Cathy. "Robert Flack, Diane Gangne." *C Magazine,* (Spring 1991).

Flack, Robert. "Art by Robert Flack." *Nouveau Midwest,* (September 1990), p.9.

Flack, Robert. "The Arts." *Avenue Magazine,* (April 1984).

Flack, Robert. "Drawings 1962–72." *Fuse,* (Summer 1991).

Flack, Robert. "The Kaleidoscopic Spyhole." (artist's project), *C Magazine,* No.7, (Fall 1985), p.33.

Flack, Robert. "Vanitas-Wheel." (artist's project), *Impulse,* No.3, (Summer 1989), p.10.

Flack, Robert. "Untitled." (self-published artist's book), Chromozone, Chromatique, Toronto, 1981.

"Goings on About Town." *The New Yorker,* (July 2, 1990), p.11.

Gagne, Diane. "The Sensory Envelope Robert Flack." *M5V,* No.2, (November 1991).

Grenville, Bruce. "Robert Flack, Cold City Gallery." *Vanguard,* Vol.17, No.4, (September/October 1987), p.35.

Hitzeroth, Connie. "Straight-shooting Split Surface." *NOW,* July 9–15, 1987.

Hoffberg, Judith. "Untitled by Robert Flack." *Umbrella Magazine,* 1982.

Holubizky, Ihor. "Genius is No Bed of Roses." *ETC Montreal,* No. 10, (Winter 1989), p.58.

Jones, Linda. "Portraits of the Psyche." *Kingston Whig-Standard,* March 26, 1988.

Lypchuk, Donna. "Transcending Matters of Sexuality in Art." *Metropolis,* July 13, 1989.

McIlroy, Randal. "Artist probes behind mascara in exploration of romance." *Winnipeg Free Press,* March 26, 1988.

McPhail, Andrew F. "Some slick, some disturbing." *Extra,* (April 1989).

O'Connor, Alan. "How Are We There." *Body Politic,* (Fall 1984).

Sorfleet, Andrew. "Homomyopia." *Fuse,* (Fall 1989), p.44.

Spalding, Linda. "Robert Flack, YYZ." *Vanguard,* (Summer 1985), p.32.

Tanguay, Pierre. "The Art of a Mental Warrior."*AIDS Action News!,* No.13, (March 1991), p.10.

Taylor, Kate. "Traditional Photography Dismantled." *The Globe and Mail,* August 2, 1991, p.C7.

LYLE ASHTON HARRIS

"The Secret Life of a Snow Queen"

I long for the relationship we used to have. Isn't it funny and paradoxical the relationship I have with myself now? All this investigating, all this theory, all this investment in how often others will perceive my work. At what point will I be able to produce work for me? At what point will I get over the fear of acknowledging my own needs? How long will I continue to play the games of mastery of the false self? When will the performance end? I long for that. They accused me of narcissism, solipsism, exhibitionism. One told me he could not understand my work because he did not grow up in a Black community. Well fuck, neither did I. Another, an instructor, frankly asked what could I expect of him since he was just a middle-class straight white guy from Santa Monica. I am the "multicultural" character personified. I guess what I fear will be exposed is that I hurt. It is not easy being one of a few "people of color" in a program with those who know very little about your culture, and do not care to know more. When they made the references to "primitive" people, "other" cultures, was it me they were referring to? Of course not. I played the game quite well. For me, it is a very fine line between falling apart and maintaining the mask, thinking any second you'll be found out. You'll be called out. To be the representative: nigger personified. In the flesh to absorb their projections, their needs, their lacks, their clandestine pleasures, their fears. Not I, for I am the quintessential Black faggot. I have learned the game all too well. I went to the right schools [that is, institutions that would validate my right to speak]. Traveled to exotic lands. Wore the right clothing for the appropriate occasions. Rolled my big brown eyes while fluidly oscillating between fem/butch positions, my version. Do I leave once again, performing the once rehearsed, now perfected, performance? One more time. And smile. You're beautiful. Has all this been my imagination?

LYLE ASHTON HARRIS
Born 1965
Lives and works in Los Angeles

EDUCATION

1991 National Graduate Photography Seminar, Tisch School of the Arts, New York, New York.

1990 MFA, California Institute of the Arts, Valencia, California.

1988 BA with departmental honours, Wesleyan University, Middletown, Connecticut.

SOLO EXHIBITIONS

1990 *The Secret Life of a Snow Queen,* Gallery 301, California Institute of the Arts, Valencia, California.

1989 *Reclaiming Sexuality,* L Shape Gallery, California. Institute of the Arts, Valencia, California.

GROUP EXHIBITIONS

1992 *Schwarze Kunst: Konzepte zu Politik und Identitat,* Neue
  Gesellschaft fur Bildende Kunst (NGBK), Berlin,
  Germany (catalogue).

1991 *Presenting Rearwards,* Rosamund Felsen Gallery,
  Los Angeles, California (catalogue).
  Someone or Somebody, Meyers/Bloom Gallery,
  Santa Monica, California.
  Reclaiming Sensuality, California Museum of
  Photography, Riverside, California.
  *Situation—Perspectives on Work by Lesbian and Gay
  Artists,* New Langton Arts, San Francisco, California.
  Blues Aesthetic, Highways Performance Space,
  Santa Monica, California.

1990 *Disputed Identities,* Camerawork, San Francisco,
  California (catalogue) Toured to Presentation House
  Gallery, Vancouver; Contemporary Arts Centre,
  New Orleans.
  AutoPortraits, Camerawork, London, England.
  AutoPortraits, The Royal National Theatre, London,
  England.

1989 *Acquired Visions: Seeing Ourselves Through AIDS,* Studio
  Museum of Harlem, New York, New York.

ARTICLES AND REVIEWS

Akomfrah, John. "On the Borderline." *Ten.8,* Vol.2, No.1,
  (Spring 1991), p.50.

"Artists explore 'Otherness'." *San Francisco Examiner,*
  November 2, 1990.

"Black Narcissus." *Newstatesman Society,* April 6, 1990. p.44.

George, Eddie. "Black Body and Public Enemy." *Ten.8,*
  Vol.2, No.1, (Spring 1991), p.68.

"In Search of a Gay Sensibility." *San Francisco Examiner,*
  June 25, 1991.

"Jeder ist eine Minderheit." *Der Tagesspiegel,* January 8,
  1992.

"L.A. Area Artists Win Four Arts Federation Fellow-
  ships." *Los Angeles Times,* July 14, 1991.

Mercer, Kobena. "Dark and Lovely: Notes on Black Gay
  Image-Making." *Ten.8,* Vol.2, No.1, (Spring 1991),
  p.78.

Ramsay, Ellen L. "Disputed Identities U.S./U.K."
  Parachute, No.65, (Spring 1992), p.59.

"'Rearwards' an Irreverent Assault on Culture."
  Los Angeles Times, August 22, 1991.

Rosenberg, Ann. "Icons of Identity." *The Vancouver Sun,*
  May 25, 1991.

"Transatlantic Otherness." *Artweek,* November 15, 1990.

Walker, Christian. "The Miscengenated Gaze." *San
  Francisco Camerawork Quarterly,* (Fall 1991), p.12.

DENIS LESSARD

Un mur d'hommes: babillard, frise, profusion. Cristallisation,
précipitation, pulvérisation. Humour.

Une réflexion que je fais d'abord pour moi-même,
homme avant d'être artiste, homme dans l'artiste, artiste
dans l'homme, et sa dimension de résonance avec l'autre
sexe. Cherchant à définir l'identité autrement que par la
seule sexualité; de même l'identité sexuelle ne saurait se
réduire au type de *pratique(s)* sexuelle(s).

Un "ensemble-atelier" où certains rapprochements sont
faits, mais dans lequel il reste encore beaucoup à faire—par
le spectateur et la spectatrice. Un désordre ordonné, l'impos-
sibilité du classement final et définitif, un sentiment d'ina-
chevé qui possède pourtant sa cohérence propre.

Une *architecture d'images* au milieu de laquelle une porte
de sortie est ménagée, pour passer à travers les images, les
modèles imposés—pour rejoindre l'autre et le féminin.

J'imagine que de tout temps, probablement, les gais ont
décontextualisé des images d'hommes, pour les admirer
tacitement, pour les re-codifier et s'en servir comme instru-
ments d'identification, de contact et de reconnaissance.

Des archives personnelles. Avec l'intention d'exposer le
pur plaisir de la recherche, de visualiser l'histoire de l'art,
spatialiser le texte qui n'a pas été fait, et ne le sera peut-être
pas—à moins qu'inversement, l'oeuvre plastique soit le nouveau point de départ, la relance du projet d'écriture . . .

Ezra Pound écrivait à Sarah Perkins Cope:

> *Skip anything you don't understand and go on till you pick
> it up again. All tosh about foreign languages making it diffi-
> cult. The quotes are all either explained at once by repeat or they
> are definitely of the things indicated. If reader don't know what
> an elefant is, then the word is obscure.*
>
> *I admit that there are a couple of Greek quotes, one along in 39
> that can't be understood without Greek, but if I can drive the
> reader to learning at least that much Greek, she or he will indu-
> bitably be filled with a durable gratitude. And if not, what harm?
> I can't conceal the fact that the Greek language existed.*

DENIS LESSARD

Born 1959
Lives and works in Montreal

EDUCATION

1985 MA, University of Montréal, Montréal, Québec.

1980 BA (Communication and Art History), Laval
  University, Québec City, Québec.

SOLO EXHIBITIONS

1991 *Displacement/Rearrangement,* Whyte Museum of the
  Canadian Rockies, Banff, Alberta.

1987 *Les fontaines,* Galerie Graff, Montréal, Québec.
 Vocabulaires, Art Actuel Acte VI, Montréal, Québec
 (catalogue).
1986 *the collections,* Ace Art Inc., Winnipeg, Manitoba.
1984 Department of Visual Arts, Ottawa University,
 Ottawa, Ontario.

GROUP EXHIBITIONS

1991 *Suivez le sens/Thread Your Way Through,* Galerie
 Barbara Silverberg, Montréal, Québec (catalogue).
1990 *Telling Things,* Art Metropole, Toronto, Ontario.
 London Life Young Contemporaries, London Regional
 Art & Historical Museums, London, Ontario.
 Touring to Mississauga Civic Centre Art Gallery,
 Mississauga, Ontario; Beaverbrook Art Gallery,
 Fredericton, New Brunswick; Mount Saint Vincent
 University, Halifax, Nova Scotia; Laurentian
 University Museum & Art Centre, Sudbury, Ontario
 (catalogue).
1989 *Séries Kompakt,* Galerie des arts Lavalin, Montréal,
 Québec (catalogue).
1988 *Scripta manent,* Galerie des arts Lavalin, Montréal,
 Québec.
 Derrière l'image: un langage, Galerie d'art du Collège
 Édouard-Montpetit, Longueuil, Québec.
 Le mot dans l'image, Centre d'exposition l'Imagier,
 Aylmer, Québec.
1986 *Absurd-e,* Galerie J. Yahouda Meir, Montréal, Québec.
 Mémoire, Art Actuel Acte VI, Montréal, Québec.
1985 *T-Shirt,* Grünwald Gallery, Toronto, Ontario.
 50 Oboro, Oboro Gallery, Montréal, Québec.
1984 *Face à Face,* Powerhouse Gallery, Montréal, Québec.
 T-Shirt, Galerie J. Yahouda Meir, Montréal, Québec.
 A la Carte, Powerhouse Gallery, Montréal, Québec.
1983 *9x9,* Galerie J. Yahouda Meir, Montréal, Québec.
 Tangente danse actuelle, Montréal, Québec.
1982 *Livres d'artistes,* La Chambre Blanche, Québec City.

BIBLIOGRAPHY

Chagnon, Johanne. "A/Venture: Les trois L en spectacle."
 Vie des Arts, No. 124, (automne 1986), p.55.
Chagnon, Johanne. "Jeux d'espace, Vieux-Port de
 Montréal." *Vanguard,* Vol.15 No.6, (December 1986/
 January 1987), p.35.
Earl, Linda. "Denis Lessard, Magpie, Alberta College of
 Art, Calgary, December 15, 1988". *The Dance connec-
 tion,* Vol.6 No.6, (January/February 1989), p.53.
Guilbert, Charles. "Objets perdus." *Voir,* Vol.1 No.23,
 (Du 7 au 13 mai 1987), p.18.
Léger, Danielle. "Aventure, Centre Saidye Bronfman."
 Vanguard, Vol.15 No.5, (October 1986). p.43.
Lupien, Jocelyne. "De la migration momentanée..." *ETC
 Montréal,* No.9, (automne 1989), p.53.
McIlroy, Randal. "Collections generate plenty of voltage."
 Winnipeg Free Press, April 5, 1986, p.25.
Sabat, Christina. "Visual Arts in Review." *The Daily
 Gleaner,* Fredericton, New Brunswick, December 1,
 1990, p.11.
Tourangeau, Jean. "Moment d'homme, volet performance,
 Tangente." *Vanguard,* Vol.14, No.2, (March 1985), p30.
Wright, Helen K. "Denis Lessard, Ace Art, Winnipeg."
 Vanguard, Vol.15, No.3, (Summer 1986), p.48.

PERFORMANCES

1991 *Reading Notes,* Whyte Museum of the Canadian
 Rockies, Banff, Alberta.
 Reading Notes: A Calgary Variation, The New Gallery,
 Calgary, Alberta.
1990 *Banff**,* Walter Phillips Art Gallery, Banff, Alberta,
 part of symposium *Voices/Voix.*
1989 *Récital, performance,* Musée d'art contemporain,
 Montréal, Québec, part of *Moments musicaux.*
1988 *Goethe,* Salle René-Provost, Hull, Québec.
 Festival La mesure des temps, Galerie Axe Néo-7,
 Hull, Québec.
 Goethe, Galerie Horace, Sherbrooke, Québec.
 Magpie, Alberta College of Art Gallery, Calgary,
 Alberta, part of the *Performance Anthology.*
1987 *Goethe,* Banff Centre, Banff, Alberta.
 Plains Canada Conference, Artspace, Winnipeg,
 Manitoba.
 Galerie Optica, Montréal, Québec.
1986 *Album,* OF Galerie, Montréal, Québec, part of
 exhibition *Aventure/Art-venture* (catalogue).
 Espace inquiet, Old Port of Montréal,
 Québec, part of exhibition *Jeux d'espace* (catalogue).
1984 *Dix petites pièces classiques,* Festival Moment d'homme,
 Tangente danse actuelle, Montréal, Québec.
 (catalogue) University of Winnipeg, Manitoba.
1983 *Les noeuds gordiens,* Tangente danse actuelle, Montréal
 Québec.

ACKNOWLEDGEMENTS

In This World: Robert Flack, Lyle Ashton Harris, Denis Lessard is an exhibition which pushes issues of male sexuality from the margins onto center stage. Flack, Harris and Lessard are three gay men whose art is about homosexual experience in a predominantly heterosexual, often hostile, society. In their own way, each of these three artists examines masculine codes—from those in the mass media to those of self-portraiture—and asks us to acknowledge how these codes are received by gay men.

The Contemporary Art Gallery is very pleased to present *In This World* and we are grateful to many who have contributed to the successful realization of this project. Keith Wallace, curator of the Contemporary Art Gallery, organized the exhibition and wrote the insightful essay which follows. Mark Budgen edited the text and Alex Hass and Barbara Hodgson designed this publication.

Our special thanks are extended to the artists, Robert Flack, Lyle Ashton Harris and Denis Lessard. They embraced the project with enthusiasm from its inception, and assisted in every phase of the exhibition's production. We are happy to have brought their work together in Vancouver.

Linda Milrod
Director

This publication is made possible with a grant from The Canada Council. Public program support has been provided by the Contemporary Art Society, Vancouver, and The Leon & Thea Koerner Foundation.